Vocabulary
in practice 4

40 units of
self-study
vocabulary
exercises

with tests

Glennis Pye

CAMBRIDGE
UNIVERSITY PRESS

PUBLISHED BY THE PRESS SYNDICATE OF THE UNIVERSITY OF CAMBRIDGE
The Pitt Building, Trumpington Street, Cambridge, United Kingdom

CAMBRIDGE UNIVERSITY PRESS
The Edinburgh Building, Cambridge CB2 2RU, UK
40 West 20th Street, New York, NY 10011–4211, USA
477 Williamstown Road, Port Melbourne, VIC 3207, Australia
Ruiz de Alarcón 13, 28014 Madrid, Spain
Dock House, The Waterfront, Cape Town 8001, South Africa

http://www.cambridge.org

First published 2003

Printed in Italy by G. Canale & C. S.p.A.

Typeface Bembo 10/11pt   *System* QuarkXpress® [HMCL]

A catalogue record for this book is available from the British Library

ISBN 0 521 75376 7

Contents

To the student

This book will give you the chance to practise your vocabulary in a fun way.

Vocabulary in Practice 4 has:
• 40 units of short, enjoyable exercises – each unit practises groups of words which belong together
• 4 Tests – one after every 10 units, helping you to remember the words from those units
• an Answer Key
• a Word List – this is a list of all the words in each unit with information about how the words are used.

You can use the book in two ways:
1 Start at the beginning of the book. Do units 1–40 and then do the Tests.
2 Look at the Contents. Do the units you think are important first. When you have finished the book, do the Tests.

You can do each unit in two ways:
1 Do the unit and check your answers in the Answer Key. Study the Word List and learn the words you got wrong. Then do the exercise again.
2 Study the Word List for the unit. Then do the unit and check your answers.

Note Do the exercises in this book in pencil. Then you can do the exercises again after a week or a month. Repeating the exercises will help you to remember the words.

Here are some ideas to help you to learn vocabulary:
• Learn groups of words which belong together [e.g. skirt, coat, trousers, etc.].
• Learn a word and also its opposite [e.g. beautiful/ugly, hot/cold].
• Draw pictures: some words are easier to remember if you draw a picture and write the word under it, e.g.

hand   spoon   fish

• Write new words in a notebook: write the meaning in English or in your own language, then write a sentence using the word.

I hope you find this book useful and that it makes learning English words fun.

1 Family

A Complete the replies on the right with the words in the box.

ex–husband   ex–wife   kids   only child
orphan   partner   triplets   twins

1   She's just had another baby, hasn't she?
    That's right. She's got four .... now.

2   Do you think you'll have another baby?
    Oh yes, I don't want Charlie to be an ....

3   Is Ray her husband?
    No, he's her .... They live together, but they're not married.

4   They got divorced three years ago, didn't they?
    Yes, Helen's his ....

5   Did you say both his parents were killed during the war?
    Yes, he's an ....

6   My sister was born just three minutes after me.
    Oh, I didn't realise you two were ....

7   You've got three babies all the same age!
    Yes, looking after .... is really hard work.

8   We were married, but I divorced him last year.
    Oh, he's your .... , then.

2 People's ages

A Use the words in the box to write sentences about which gift to buy for each person.

adult   baby
~~child~~   teenager
toddler

 Melanie   Anne-Sophie   Gary   Nicola    Gianni

1 LEARN-TO-WRITE GAME
2 RATTLE
3 TRICYCLE
4 TRAINERS
5 THEATRE TICKETS

1 *Buy the learn-to-write game for Anne-Sophie – she's a child.*

2 ....

3 ....

4 ....

5 ....

B Complete the sentences with the words in the box.

birth   childhood   ~~death~~   early   late
middle-aged   old age   teens   twenties

1 (died aged 99) He was 99 at the time of his ......*death*...... .

2 (age: 13→19) She was in her .... when she went abroad for the first time.

3 (age: 37→39) He only got married in his .... thirties.

4 (age: 50) He's ....

5 (age: 0) At the time of my .... , my parents were living in London.

6 (age: 20→29) He learnt to drive when he was in his ....

7 (age: 0→12) He had a very happy ....

8 (age: 41→43) She was in her .... forties when she had her third child.

9 (age: 65+) I save money so that I'll be able to live comfortably in my

....

3 Describing character 1

A Look at the pictures. Complete Ed and Kate's lists about who they would or would not choose as their new flatmate.

Ed

I like   I would choose

1 people who enjoy laughing   ....Maxine.........
   a lot
2 people who always try to do   ....
   their job well
3 people who want to be successful   ....
4 people who are good at   ....
   learning and understanding things

I don't like   I wouldn't choose

5 people who think they're   ....
   better than other people
6 people who don't talk much   ....

Jake – serious,
slightly arrogant

Simon – hard-working,
very organized

Maxine – has a good
sense of humour,
easy-going

Kate

I like   I would choose

7 people who are relaxed and   ....
   don't get upset easily
8 people who are sure they can   ....
   do things well
9 people who like to do things   ....
   to show their love for someone
10 people who plan things well   ....
   and don't waste time

I don't like   I wouldn't choose

11 people who don't laugh much   ....
12 people who never want help, ...
   but like to do things themselves

Jerry – confident,
ambitious

Dominic – intelligent,
romantic

Lily – quiet,
independent

4 Describing character 2

Find six adjectives for describing character in the grid. Then match the words with the definitions.

i	m	m	a	t	u	r	e	t	w
x	l	o	z	c	g	e	q	y	c
p	s	d	w	r	c	h	d	u	r
o	d	e	h	f	h	g	t	i	e
m	f	s	t	l	a	f	j	p	a
a	r	t	u	n	r	d	n	l	t
t	y	y	i	b	m	s	i	k	i
u	f	m	d	f	i	z	r	b	v
r	e	a	s	o	n	a	b	l	e
e	j	n	i	a	g	m	h	o	c

1 behaving in a silly way, like a younger person ....
2 good at using your imagination and thinking of new ideas ....
3 very pleasant ....
4 fair and showing good judgement ....
5 sensible, like an adult ....
6 not talking in a proud way about yourself and the good things you have done ....

B **Match the words in the box with what the people are saying.**

loyal optimistic pessimistic sensitive sociable vain

1 I love spending time with people and meeting new people. ....
2 I always support my friends even when they're having difficult times. ....
3 I always try to think about how other people feel. ....
4 I always think good things are going to happen. ....
5 I always think bad things are going to happen. ....
6 I look so beautiful, don't I? ....

5 How you feel

A Circle the correct word in each sentence.

1 I'm confused / satisfied. Everyone I ask about it tells me something different.

2 I'm very disappointed / nervous. I've got to stand up and talk in front of 300 people.

3 I just feel so depressed / relieved. I have no money, no friends and nowhere to live.

4 I'm frustrated / shocked. A friend of the family has been arrested for murder!

5 I'm so excited / stressed. My best friend is coming and we haven't seen each other for ten years.

6 I'm very homesick / upset. She just suddenly started shouting at me.

B Complete the sentences with the other words from A.

1 I feel .... I'm very busy at work and I'm studying for an exam in my spare time. I just don't have any time to relax.

2 I feel so .... She really needs my help, but there's nothing I can do.

3 I'm a little .... I haven't seen my friends and family for such a long time.

4 I'm so .... you're here. I was beginning to think you'd had an accident.

5 I'm really .... We've had to cancel our skiing holiday because John's broken his leg.

6 I'm not .... with the repair work they've done in my house. It's just not good enough.

6 Love and marriage

A **Read what the people are saying. Then match the words in the box with the correct person.**

> divorced   married   separated   single   widowed

1   I'm Patrick. My ex-wife's name is Valerie.   ....

2   I'm Freya. I'm not married.   ....

3   I'm Guy. My wife and I don't live together any more.   ....

4   I'm Lena. My husband's name is Lars.   ....

5   I'm Jacques. My wife died ten years ago.   ....

B **Complete the paragraph with the words in the box. Remember to put the verbs in the correct form.**

> an affair   fancy   go out with   live with
> relationship   romantic   split up

I'd (1) .... Kyoko for a long time; I thought she had such beautiful eyes and I loved the way she laughed. When I first met her, she was (2) .... someone else. They'd been together for about three years and seemed very happy, so I thought it wasn't likely that their (3) .... would end. Then I heard that her boyfriend had been seeing another woman. When Kyoko found out that he'd been having (4) ...., she told him it was finished and they (5) .... Not long after that, Kyoko and I started seeing each other. Now I'm (6) .... her in a flat that we bought together. Next week I'm planning to take her to a restaurant for a (7) .... dinner and I'm going to ask her to marry me.

7 Your body

A Circle the correct word on the right for each definition.

1 the long thing down the centre of your back which supports your body   ribs / (spine)

2 something which becomes longer or shorter to make a part of your body move and which you can make stronger by doing exercises   heart / muscle

3 the hair above your eye   eyebrow / eyelashes

4 the inside part of your hand   palm / spine

5 the outside part of your whole body   bone / skin

6 the short hairs that grow from the edge of the part that covers your eye   eyelashes / eyelid

7 one of the hard pieces in your body   bone / brain

8 the thing that covers your eye   eyebrow / eyelid

9 the things in your body that you breathe with   lungs / skin

10 the thing inside your head that controls how you think and move   brain / palm

11 the hard curved pieces that surround your chest and protect what is inside your chest   lungs / ribs

12 the thing in your chest that pumps blood around your body   heart / muscle

B Complete the sentences with words from A.

1 She held the insect in the .... of her hand.

2 One of the players pulled a .... in his back when he was trying to score a goal.

3 The ball hit him right in the eye and his .... was badly swollen.

4 The .... on my face is beginning to get lines on it now that I'm a bit older.

5 It looks like he might need an operation on his .... to cure his back problem.

6 My sister broke a .... in her foot when she was playing tennis.

8 The senses

A Complete the word webs with the words in the box.

> hear   listen   look   noise   see   sight   sound   watch

hearing
- noun
  - **1** a s..
  - **2** a ....
- verb
  - **3** l..
  - **4** ....

sight
- noun
  - **5** a ....
- verb
  - **6** s..
  - **7** l..
  - **8** ....

B The underlined words are in the wrong sentences. Write the correct word for each sentence.

1 Hold your nose so that you can't <u>touch</u> it.   ....

2 Don't <u>taste</u> that – it'll break.   ....

3 <u>Smell</u> this – it's really smooth.   ....

4 This sauce has a really bitter <u>smell</u>.   ....

5 This jumper <u>smells</u> really smooth.   ....

6 <u>Feel</u> this – it's really sweet.   ....

7 Don't drink that water – it <u>feels</u> horrible.   ....

8 This cheese <u>tastes</u> horrible, but you should try it – it's delicious.   ....

9 There's a delicious <u>taste</u> of cooking coming from the kitchen.   ....

9 Driving a car

A The <u>underlined</u> words are in the wrong sentences. Write the correct word for each sentence.

1 The <u>brake</u> is the part of a car that you press with your foot to change gear. ....

2 The <u>driving test</u> is the part of a car that starts the engine. ....

3 The <u>accelerator</u> is the part of a car you press with your foot to make it go slower or stop. ....

4 A <u>clutch</u> is an official document that allows you to drive a car. ....

5 The <u>ignition</u> is the part of a car that you press with your foot to make it go faster. ....

6 A <u>driving licence</u> is an official examination that you have to pass to be able to drive. ....

B Complete the paragraph with the words in the box.

change gear   indicate   in first gear   in neutral   move off
overtake   park   reverse   slow down   speed up   start up

Before you switch on the engine, fasten your seatbelt and check that the

car is (1) .... Now you can (2) .... the

engine by putting the key in the ignition and turning it. Put the car

(3) .... , check in your mirrors to see that no other cars

are coming and (4) .... slowly. (5) .... by

pressing your foot down on the accelerator and remember to

(6) .... If you want to (7) .... another car,

check in your mirrors and (8) .... to show that you are

moving out. To (9) .... , press your foot down on the

brake. When you arrive at your destination, you should look for somewhere

to (10) .... the car. To do this, it is sometimes easier to

(11) .... the car into the space, but remember to check in

your mirrors before you start moving backwards.

10 Signs

A Write the words in the box in the correct place.

delayed   do not bend   do not disturb   for sale   fragile   no entry
nothing to declare   on time   out of order   reserved   sale   to let

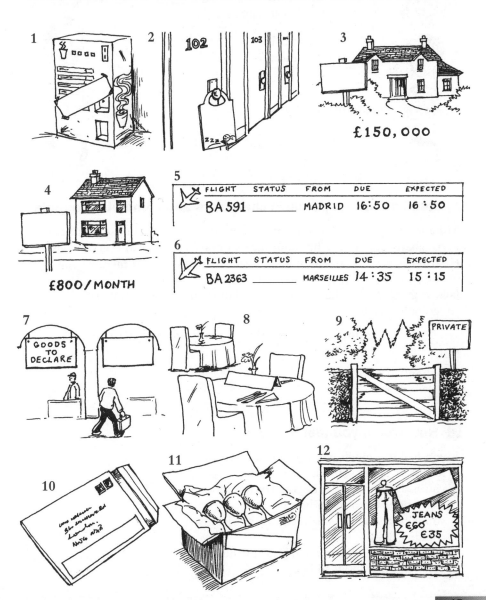

£150,000

£800/MONTH

FLIGHT	STATUS	FROM	DUE	EXPECTED
BA 591	_____	MADRID	16:50	16:50

FLIGHT	STATUS	FROM	DUE	EXPECTED
BA 2363	_____	MARSEILLES	14:35	15:15

GOODS TO DECLARE

PRIVATE

JEANS €60 €35

Test 1 (Units 1–10)

A Follow the lines. Then complete what the people are saying.

1 My brother and I were born on the same day 38 years ago.   We're ....

2 I'm not married to him any more.   He's my ....
He's in ....

3 I'm not married to her any more.   He's my ....

4 We live together, but we're not married. We're both 45.   We're ....
We're in ....

B Read about the people's characters and complete the table.

Mike is very good at learning and understanding things, but sometimes he starts talking about how he thinks he's so much better than everyone else.
Heather is very relaxed and doesn't get upset easily, but sometimes she spends too much time looking at herself in the mirror.
Jack is great at thinking up new ideas, but then he always thinks bad things are going to happen.

	good characteristic	bad characteristic
Mike	....	....
Heather	....	....
Jack	....	....

C How would you feel if ... ?

1 you had too much work to do and no time to rest or enjoy yourself   ....

2 you had been in another country for a long time and wanted to go home   ....

3 you kept trying to do something, but just couldn't do it   ....

4 you were five years old and your birthday party was just about to begin   ....

D Label the pictures with words for parts of the body.

1 ....
2 ....
3 ....

4 ....
5 ....

E Complete the sentences with the correct words.

1 You'll have to speak louder. My .... isn't too good these days.

2 You go and play. I'll sit here and .... you.

3 Stop making that .... I'm trying to think.

4 Can you .... the scissors anywhere? I know they're here somewhere.

F Complete the sentences about driving a car.

1 He's .... his car.

2 He's .... another car.

3 He's .... the car.

4 He's .... to turn right.

G What sign do you see if ... ?

1 something is broken and you cannot use it

....

2 a train or plane is not late

....

3 a shop is selling things at lower prices than usual

....

4 a table in a restaurant is being kept for someone

....

11 Television

Look at the programme schedule. Complete the sentences with the words in the box.

cartoon chat show documentary game show soap opera the news

5.30	**Polly Pet** One for the little ones – Polly Pet gets into trouble again.	
6.00	**The World at Six** A look at what's been happening at home and abroad.	
7.00	**Devon Doorways** Tonight's episode sees Marcia falling out with just about everyone else in the village.	
8.00	**Here and Now** This week's programme looks at world climate change.	
9.00	**In the Chair** This week's guest is megastar Ben Polance, interviewed by the king of questions.	
9.30	**Beginner's Luck** Who will win the big prize in tonight's challenge?	

1 At half past five, there's
a ....

2 At six o'clock, there's
....

3 At seven o'clock, there's
a ....

4 At eight o'clock, there's
a ....

5 At nine o'clock, there's
a ....

6 At half past nine, there's
a ....

B **Join the people with what they are saying.**

1
viewer

My first guest tonight is the actor and singer, Joel Williams.

2
newsreader

Tonight we are going to look at crime in our cities and what's being done about it.

3
presenter

I'll be back tomorrow with the nine o'clock news, so until then, goodnight.

4
chat show host

Now, what shall I watch tonight?

12 Cinema

A Match the pictures with the words in the box.

action film   animated film   comedy   horror film
science fiction film   thriller   war film   western

1 ....
2 ....
3 ....
4 ....
5 ....
6 ....
7 ....
8 ....

B Label the picture with the words in the box.

actor   actress   cameraman   costume designer   director
film star   make-up artist   producer

1 ....
2 ....
3 ....
4 ....
5 ....
6 ....
7 ....
8 ....

13 Newspapers and magazines

A **Read the descriptions and write the words from the box in the word web.**

> a broadsheet a daily a local newspaper
> a national newspaper a tabloid a weekly

published every day	1	*a daily*
news about one area of a country	2	
large pages, serious news	3	
newspaper — published once a week	4	
news about the whole country	5	
small pages, lots of pictures, not much serious news	6	

B **Match the pairs of sentences.**

1 (I'm in charge of a newspaper or magazine.) He's a member of the paparazzi. ☐

2 (I write articles about news.) She's an editor. ☐

3 (I follow and take photos of famous people.) He's a reporter. ☐

C **Find the first letter of each word. Match the words with the definitions.**

1 the title of a story printed in large letters on the front of a newspaper ....

2 a piece of writing ....

3 newspapers and magazines, or the people who write for them ....

4 a long piece of writing on a special subject in a newspaper or magazine ....

14 Books

A **Write the type of book each person should take off the shelf.**

1 I'd like to know which museums I should go to see when I'm on holiday. ....

2 I'm not sure what this word means. ....

3 I'm not sure how you make apple pie. ....

4 I'm not sure which countries are next to Poland. ....

5 I need to find out about what it was like when dinosaurs lived on Earth. ....

6 I need to do some exercises to improve my English vocabulary. ....

7 I want to know all about her life. ....

8 I'm not sure how to load this software. ....

9 I love reading stories told with pictures. ....

10 I want to read about something that isn't real. ....

11 I'd like to know what he thought about all the things that happened to him in his life. ....

B **The <u>underlined</u> words are in the wrong sentences. Write the correct word for each sentence.**

1 A <u>chapter</u> is a book that has a thick, stiff cover. ....

2 A <u>hardback</u> is a person in a book. ....

3 A <u>character</u> is one of the parts that a book is divided into. ....

4 The <u>author</u> of a book is its name. ....

5 A <u>title</u> is a book that has a thin paper cover. ....

6 The <u>paperback</u> of a book is the person who has written it. ....

15 Cooking

A Look at the pictures and complete the sentences. Remember to use the past tense form of the verbs.

1 I didn't boil the egg. I .... it.
2 I didn't fry the chicken. I .... it.
3 I didn't bake the peas. I .... them.
4 I didn't grill the cake. I .... it.
5 I didn't roast the fish. I .... it.

B Circle the correct word in each sentence.

1

Chop / Peel the onion.

2

Slice / Grate the cheese.

3

Spread / Squeeze the lemon.

4

Slice / Chop the tomato.

5

Grate / Spread the butter.

6

Peel / Squeeze the potatoes.

16 The taste of food

A Complete what the people are saying with the words in the box.

bitter   sour   spicy   sweet

1   This is a bit too .... for me!

2   Oh, that's so ....

3   Mmm, lots of sugar! This is really ....

4   Yuk! This milk is ....

B Match the plates of food with the people who ate them. Write the letters in the box below.

1   Mine didn't have a very strong taste.

2   There was a lot of salt in mine.

3   Mine tasted great.

4   Mine didn't have any taste at all.

5   There was a lot of cream and butter in mine.

6   Mine tasted really bad.

a   DELICIOUS
b   RICH
c   HORRIBLE
d   SALTY
e   MILD
f   TASTELESS

1 ....   2 ....   3 ....   4 ....   5 ....   6 ....

17 Sounds

A Label the pictures with the words in the box.

| bang | buzz | crackle | creak | crunch | fizz | pop | ring | sizzle | splash |

1 ....
2 ....
3 ....
4 ....
5 ....
6 ....
7 ....
8 ....
9 ....
10 ....

B Complete the sentences with the verbs from A. Remember to use the correct form of the verbs.

1 Be careful, Jasmine. There's a bee .... around your head.

2 Mummy, I'm .... you! Are you wet?

3 Listen to how this apple .... when I bite into it.

4 The cork .... as she opened the champagne.

5 .... the bell and see if anyone is at home.

6 Let the sausages .... in the pan, turning them until they are brown all over.

7 Can you please stop .... that drum – it's giving me a headache.

8 Wait till it stops .... before you try to drink it.

9 Don't step on that stair – it ....

10 I love the way the wood .... as it burns.

18 Home technology

A Use the words in the box to make new words.

alarm	camera	clock	control	dish
phone	player	player	player	TV

1 burglar ....
2 CD ....
3 cordless ....
4 digital ....
5 DVD ....

6 minidisc ....
7 radio-alarm ....
8 remote ....
9 satellite ....
10 widescreen ....

B Label the pictures with the new words from A.

1 ....
2 ....
3 ....
4 ....
5 ....
6 ....
7 ....
8 ....
9 ....
10 ....

C Complete the sentences with words from A.

1 This .... is great! I can talk into it and walk around the house at the same time.

2 This .... is great! The picture and sound quality are excellent.

3 This .... is great! I can listen to my music on the train and it's so small it fits in my handbag.

4 This .... is great! It wakes me up with music every morning.

5 This .... is great! I can delete the awful photos and save the ones I want to keep on my computer.

6 This .... is great! I don't have to leave my chair when I want to change channel on the TV.

19 The environment

A Use the words in the box to make new words.

| effect   fumes   layer   rain   warming   waste |

1 ozone ....
2 global ....
3 greenhouse ....
4 nuclear ....
5 exhaust ....
6 acid ....

B Match the new words from A with the definitions.

1 the unwanted gases, etc. that are produced when ....
   making nuclear power

2 the gas that comes from a vehicle's engine ....

3 a type of oxygen around the Earth that stops ....
   the sun from harming the Earth

4 water that falls from the sky and contains ....
   chemicals that damage plants, etc.

5 the way in which the Earth is slowly getting ....
   warmer because gases are stopping heat from
   leaving it

6 the way in which the Earth's weather is getting ....
   warmer because of pollution

C Complete the paragraph with the words in the box.
   Remember to use the correct form of the verbs.

| organic   pesticides   pollute   pollution   recycle   recycling |

SAVING OUR ENVIRONMENT

Our environment is in trouble. Modern ways of living and today's
industries are (1) .... it. Most people think there is nothing
they can do. This is not true. Everyone can do something to help save our
environment. Here's a list of things you can do.

– Help to cut (2) .... by taking the bus to work instead
  of your car.

– Buy (3) .... fruit and vegetables that have not been
  treated with (4) ....

– (5) .... all your cans, bottles and paper. There should be a
  (6) .... centre somewhere near your home, so take them there.

20 Natural disasters

A Label the pictures with the words in the box.

> avalanche   drought   earthquake   flood
> forest fire   hurricane   volcanic eruption

1 ....
2 ....
3 ....
4 ....
5 ....
6 ....
7 ....

B Complete the paragraph with the words in the box.

> casualties   death toll   rescue operation   rescue workers
> state of emergency   survivors   victims

EARTHQUAKE DISASTER

It is now feared that the (1) .... following yesterday's
earthquake could be as high as 3,000. Many of the (2) ....
died when their homes collapsed. The government has declared a
(3) .... and is organizing a massive (4) ....
(5) .... are searching for (6) .... still
trapped under the rubble, although it is now unlikely there will be any
more (7) ....

A Complete the sentences with words for TV programmes and films which mean the same as the words in brackets.

1 I watched a .... (interview with famous actor)

2 I watched a .... (funny film)

3 I watched a .... (people trying to win prizes)

4 I watched a .... (film with cowboys)

5 I watched a .... (very frightening film)

6 I watched a .... (programme with facts about a situation)

B Complete the sentences with words for newspapers and books.

1 I don't want to read too much serious news when I'm on holiday, so I sometimes buy a ....

2 I'm reading a great .... at the moment. It's a story about a woman who starts to imagine she's changing into an animal.

3 We get the .... It's got all sorts of interesting information in it about things that are happening in the area I live in.

4 If you don't know where Majorca is, look it up in an ....

C Complete the cooking instructions.

1 .... an onion and .... it into very small pieces. Next, ... it in a frying pan in just a little oil.

2 Take some chicken pieces and .... some lemon juice over them. Add a little salt and pepper, and .... the chicken in the oven for about 45 minutes.

3 Fill a large pan with water. Wait for the water to .... before adding the pasta. When the pasta is cooked, pour the sauce onto it and simply .... some of your favourite cheese over it.

Test 2 (Units 11–20)

D **Complete the sentences with words to describe the taste of food.**

1 There's too much lemon in this. It tastes ....
2 There's too much sugar in this. It's too ....
3 There's a lot of pepper in this. It's very ....
4 There aren't many spices in this. It's very ....
5 There's a lot of butter and cream in this. It's very ....
6 There's too much salt in this. It's too ....

E **Circle the correct word for each sentence.**

1 He fizzed / banged / splashed on the door with his fist.
2 The bacon rang / creaked / sizzled in the pan.
3 There was a loud buzz / pop / splash as she landed in the water.
4 The old bed creaked / buzzed / rang as he lay down on it.
5 There was a loud crunch / splash / pop as the tyre burst.

F **Label the pictures with words for home technology.**

1   2   3   4

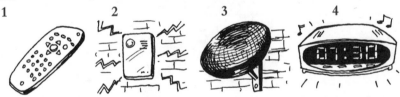

....

....

G **Write the words for the definitions.**

1 the people who try to help the people who are affected by a disaster ....
2 a storm with very strong winds ....
3 damage caused by harmful chemicals to the air, water, etc. ....
4 using things again instead of throwing them away ....
5 a word which describes food that has not been treated with chemicals ....
6 the people who do not die in a disaster ....

29

21 Studying at university

A Complete what the people are saying with the words in the box.

agriculture   architecture   business studies   engineering
journalism   law   medicine   modern languages   politics

1 I studied ....

2 I studied ....

3 I studied ....

4 I studied ....

5 I studied ....

6 I studied ....

7 I studied ....

8 I studied ....

9 I studied ....

B Find the first letter of the words. Match the words with the definitions.

1 someone who is studying at university   ....

2 someone who teaches at a university   ....

3 a qualification that you get when you
  finish university   ....

4 a talk on a subject given by a teacher
  at a university to a large group of people   ....

5 a class at university where a small
  group of people and their teacher
  discuss a subject   ....

22 Crime

A Match the pairs of sentences. Write the letters in the box below.

1 Jack Jones took things from a shop without paying.
2 Ben Walsh killed someone.
3 Les Bickerton bombed a building because of what he believed in.
4 Kenneth Green got into a house and took all the jewellery.

a He was arrested for murder.
b He was arrested for shoplifting.
c He was arrested for burglary.
d He was arrested for terrorism.

| 1 .... | 2 .... | 3 .... | 4 .... |

B Complete the sentences about the people in A with the words in the box.

burglar   murderer   shoplifter   terrorist

1 Jack Jones is a ....
2 Ben Walsh is a ....
3 Les Bickerton is a ....
4 Kenneth Green is a ....

C Complete the paragraph with the words in the box. Remember to put the verbs in the correct form.

arrest   burglary   break into   commit   criminals   steal   victims

MAN FINALLY CAUGHT

Police investigating the (1) .... of ten homes in the
Richmond area have (2) .... a local man. The man was
caught as he (3) .... a house in St Margaret's Road. The
owner of the house believes he may have been trying to get into the
house to (4) .... a valuable collection of paintings
which she owns. Police think he is likely to be part of a gang of
(5) .... who have been (6) .... crimes all over
the area recently. PC Kirkland said, 'The (7) ....
of these crimes often suffer from stress for a long time after the event.'

23 Law and justice

A Label the picture with the words in the box.

court   judge   jury   lawyer

1 ....

2 ....

3 ....

4 ....

B Match the pairs of sentences. Write the letters in the box below.

1 What? They arrested him?

2 Who arrested him?

3 They said they had a witness.

4 I suppose he said he didn't do it.

5 Do they have any other evidence?

6 Do you think he's guilty?

7 30 years?

8 It must be terrible being in prison.

a Well, they said they found some of his hair in her house.

b What? Someone who saw him do it?

c Yes. They took him to the police station to ask him some questions because they think he might have killed her.

d The police, of course.

e Yes, I'm sure he's the one who did it.

f Yes, imagine being kept in a place and not being able to leave.

g Yes, it's long, but that's the sort of sentence you get for murder.

h That's right. He said he was innocent.

1 .... 2 .... 3 .... 4 .... 5 .... 6 .... 7 .... 8 ....

24 Getting a job

A Circle the word on the right for each definition.

1 a meeting in which someone asks you questions to see if you are suitable for a job   interview / reference

2 the money you are paid for doing a job   apply / salary

3 money your company pays you when you are old and have stopped working for them   pension / salary

4 a list of printed questions from a company that you answer to try to get a job with them   application form / experience

5 a car or health insurance, for example, that you get from your company as well as your pay   benefits / CV

6 an announcement in a newspaper, etc. which invites people to apply for a job   advertisement / interview

7 something you get when you pass an exam or finish a course of study   benefits / qualifications

8 a letter written by someone who knows you to say that you are suitable for a job   pension / reference

9 to officially ask for a job   apply / vacancy

10 a job that is available for someone to do   advertisement / vacancy

11 knowledge or skills that you get from doing a job   experience / qualifications

12 a document with information about jobs you have done and exams you have passed which you send to a company you want to work for   application form / CV

B Complete the paragraph with words from A.

ADMINISTRATION OFFICER

We have a (1) .... for an administration officer to work in our busy Sheffield office. If you have a minimum of two years (2) .... in this sort of work and enjoy being part of a team, send for an (3) .... to the address below. (4) .... is in the region of £12,000, depending on (5) .... (Those with university degrees may receive more.) Other (6) .... include the use of the company gym and subsidised meals in the staff restaurant. (7) .... will be held on November 5th and 6th at our London office.

25 Talking about your work

A Complete the sentences with the words in the box.

as   do   for   in

1

What do you ....?

2

I work .... a nurse in a large children's hospital.

3

I work .... a company which sells farm machinery.

4

I work .... the tourist industry.

B Complete the paragraphs with the words in the box.

earning	employed	from home	long hours	made redundant
pay rise	permanent	promoted	set up	temporary	the office
training	unemployed			

I've been (1) .... by my present company for two years now.
I came here straight after finishing university. I was really pleased because I
was (2) .... some money at last. The company has an
excellent (3) .... programme and so I knew I would learn
my job properly. I sometimes have to work (4) .... – I didn't
get home till after nine o'clock yesterday. But it's possible for me to work
(5) .... sometimes too – I have a computer in my spare
room. It's good to get away from (6) .... now and again, and
I find I can get a lot done when there's no one else around.

   Now that I've been here two years, I'm hoping I'll be (7) ....
soon – that should also mean I'll get a (8) .... and it'd be
nice to have a bit more money. In the future I'd like to (9) ....
my own business, but I'll stay here for now. One of my friends is
(10) .... at the moment and can't find a job anywhere. He was
(11) .... last year. Luckily, he's been able to find
(12) .... work – he's worked for several different companies
for a few months each time. But he'd prefer to work for just one and so he's
hoping to find a (13) .... job very soon.

26 Who works in a company

A Complete what the people are saying with the words in the box.

accounts manager   boss   chief executive   managing director
personal assistant   personnel manager   receptionist   secretary
sales manager   sales representative

1   I'm Peter Stent. I'm the .... here and I'm in charge of all the people who sell our products.

2   I'm the .... I'm responsible for finding people to work for this company.

3   I'm a .... I travel around the country selling the company's products. Peter Stent is my ....

4   I'm the .... I'm in charge of all the money the company makes and spends.

5   I'm Kate Derby, ... and .... I'm in charge of this company.

6   I'm a .... My job is to welcome people as they come into the company's building.

7   I'm Kate Derby's .... As head of the company, she's a very busy woman. I arrange all her meetings, make telephone calls and write letters for her, as well as all sorts of other things.

8   I'm a .... I do lots of things in my job, such as arranging meetings, making telephone calls and writing letters.

27 Money

A Join the beginnings and endings of the words. Then write the words.

1 bi	**ges**	1 .... *bills* ....
2 wa	*gage*	2 ....
3 mort	**lls**	3 ....
4 re	*rest*	4 ....
5 inte	**xes**	5 ....
6 ta	**nt**	6 ....

B Complete the sentences with the words from A.

1 We all pay .... to help pay for schools, hospitals, police officers, etc.

2 I'd like to buy a house, so I need to get a ....

3 I pay £300 .... a month for a room in a house that I share with three other people.

4 Don't forget, you'll have .... to pay for things like gas and electricity.

5 I have to go to the office every week to collect my ....

6 If you borrow money from the bank, you have to pay them

....

C Complete the crossword.

1 money that a company loses
2 having very little money
3 to have to give someone money back because you borrowed money from them
4 money that you spend when you are doing your job that you get back from your company
5 money that a company makes by selling things for more than it cost them to make
6 to have enough money to pay for something
7 having a lot of money

28 Using a computer

A Find ten computer words in the grid. Then complete the words in the list.

p	d	e	l	e	t	e	g	o	r
a	p	l	m	x	r	p	z	p	q
s	h	j	a	c	o	p	y	e	u
t	c	u	t	v	e	r	m	n	l
e	l	d	a	c	r	b	x	o	s
f	o	r	q	e	d	i	t	z	a
e	s	p	u	x	c	s	y	n	v
y	e	d	r	i	a	i	w	p	e
p	r	i	n	t	g	k	l	s	z

1 d _ _ _ _ _
2 o _ _ _
3 c _ _ _ _
4 e d _ _
5 e x _ _
6 s _ _ _
7 c _ _ _
8 p a _ _ _
9 c _ _
10 p r _ _ _

B Use words from A to label the computer icons.

1  2   3   4

....

C Use the words in the box to complete the sentences.

1   2   3   4

click   highlight   key   scroll

1 .... the words you want to delete.
2 .... down to the end of the page.
3 .... on 'file'.
4 Press any ....

29 Politics

A **Complete the definitions with the words in the box.**

> government   ministers   politicians   president / prime minister

1 people who represent the country in parliament ....

2 the political party that controls the country ....

3 the leader of the political party that controls the country ....

4 other important people in the political party that controls the country ....

B **Complete the paragraph with the words in the box. Remember to put the verbs in the correct form.**

> be in power   candidates   elect   hold an election
> policies   political party   vote for

HOW WE CHOOSE OUR LEADERS

In a democratic country where the people choose their leaders, this is done by (1).. Everyone in the country can (2).. the person they think would make the best leader. There are usually several (3).. who hope to be (4).. as leader. They try to persuade people to choose them by travelling around the country talking about the things they believe in – about the (5).. they would create if they became leader. Most leaders are members of a (6).. and, when chosen by the people, they will (7).. for a number of years.

30 War and peace

A **Look at the picture. Complete the sentences with the words in the box.**

| ally army civilians enemy prisoners |

1 This man is a soldier. He's a member of his country's ....
2 This soldier is fighting against soldier 1. His country is the ....
   of soldier 1's country.
3 This soldier is from another country. He is fighting with soldier 1 against
   soldier 2. Soldier 3's country is an .... of soldier 1's country.
4 These people are .... They have been caught.
5 These people are not soldiers. They are ....

B **Complete the paragraph with the words in the box.
Remember to put the verbs in the correct form.**

| attack capture ceasefire declare
| defend invade peace talks retreat |

WAR BETWEEN SPERLAND AND POTRINIA

In the early hours of yesterday morning soldiers from
Sperland (1) .... Potrinia, despite
warnings from the Potrinian government not to come
onto their territory. They (2) ....
villages just across the border. Village leaders were (3) .... and
taken back to Sperland as prisoners. Villagers tried to (4) ....
their homes, but few had weapons and most were forced to
(5) .... to safer areas away from the border. Following these
events, Potrinia (6) .... war on Sperland. Neighbours of the
two countries have called for a (7) .... One said, 'There
must be an end to all fighting.' It is hoped that the Sperlish and Potrinian
leaders will agree to meet some time next week for (8) ....

A Complete the sentences with words for university subjects.

1 I want to be a doctor, so I'm going to study ....
2 I want to be a farmer, so I'm going to study ....
3 I want to build roads and bridges, so I'm going to study ....
4 I want to write for a newspaper, so I'm going to study ....
5 I want to teach French and Spanish, so I'm going to study ....
6 I want to be a judge, so I'm going to study ....

B Match the pairs of sentences. Write the letters in the box below.

1 I steal things from people's houses.	a He's a murderer.
2 I committed a crime because of what I believe in.	b He's a criminal.
3 I decide how long someone should go to prison for.	c He's a burglar.
4 I've committed many crimes.	d He's a judge.
5 I saw a crime happening.	e He's a witness.
6 I killed someone.	f He's a terrorist.

1	2	3	4	5	6 ....

C Rewrite what Karen is saying about her job. Complete the sentences so that they have the same meaning.

I'm Karen Stirling. I have a job with a large company.
I'm the person in charge of all the people who sell the
company products. I used to be one of the people who
travelled around selling the products, but I was given this
better job last year. Some of my friends don't have jobs,
so I think I'm very lucky. What's your job?

I'm Karen Stirling. I (1) .... a large company. I'm the
(2) .... I used to be a (3) .... , but I was
(4) .... last year. Some of my friends are (5) .... ,
so I think I'm very lucky. What do (6) .... ?

Test 3 (Units 21–30)

D Rewrite what Richard is saying. Complete the sentences so that they have the same meaning.

I'm Richard Moss. I'm at university, but I have just written to a company to get a job. I read about the job in the local newspaper, so I wrote a letter and sent a list of all the qualifications and work experience I have. Now I'm waiting to see if they invite me to a meeting to ask me questions to see if I am suitable for the job. I'd like a good amount of money for the job because I want my own house and will have borrowed money to buy it.

I'm Richard Moss. I'm at university, but I have just (1) .... a job with a company. I saw an (2) .... for the job in the local newspaper, so I wrote a letter and sent my (3) .... Now I'm waiting to see if I get an (4) .... I'd like a good (5) .... because I want my own house and I'll have a (6) ....

E Put the letters in order to find ten computer words.

1 p y o c	....	6 v s e a	....
2 h g i l h i t h g	....	7 e t l e d e	....
3 s t e a p	....	8 d i t e	....
4 l o c s r l	....	9 t u c	....
5 i n r p t	....	10 t x e i	....

F Write who the people are.

1 I work in politics. ....

2 I've been captured by the enemy army. ....

3 I'm hoping that people will vote for me. ....

4 I'm not a soldier. ....

5 I have an important position in the government. ....

31 Talking about language

A Complete the sentences with the words in the box.

accent adjectives adverbs formal grammar informal
nouns pronunciation translate verbs vocabulary

1 You can study .... rules from a book, but you can only learn to speak English by speaking.

2 You can use .... like 'happily' and 'well' to describe how you do something.

3 My sister doesn't know any English, so I'm going to .... the story for her.

4 I find it quite difficult to understand her because she has a very strong Spanish ....

5 It's OK to use .... language if you're speaking to a friend.

6 Learning .... is very important. If you don't know the correct words, you won't be able to communicate very well.

7 .... are words which describe objects or states, like 'dictionary' and 'happiness'.

8 You can use .... like 'miserable' and 'smooth' to describe what someone or something is like.

9 .... is important – if you can't say a word properly people might not understand you.

10 People usually use more .... language when they're in serious situations like interviews.

11 We use .... like 'run' and 'smile' to talk about actions.

B Which question should each person ask? Rewrite what they are saying with the questions in the box.

What does ... mean? How do you spell ... ?
How do you pronounce ... ?

1 I know how to say 'sociable', but I don't know how to write it. ....

2 I don't understand the word 'muscle'. ....

3 I don't know how to say 'squeeze'. ....

32 Expressions of time

A Circle the correct word in each expression of time.

1 at / (for) ages
2 in / now and then
3 no / these days
4 so / these far
5 at / for last
6 no / on longer
7 from / so now on
8 at / from once
9 at / no the moment
10 in / now time
11 on / so time

B Complete the sentences with the words from A.

1 I don't usually eat sweets, but .... I like to have a bar of chocolate.

2 There's a fire – you must leave the building ....

3 If we hurry, we'll be there .... to see her before she goes home.

4 I was pleased – the train arrived ...., so I wasn't late for my meeting.

5 I'm busy ...., but I'll be able to help you when I've finished this.

6 He was 92 years old and could .... see or hear very well.

7 We haven't seen them .... We don't seem to be able to find the time to visit each other.

8 I've been trying to do this crossword for three hours and .... I've only got one of the answers.

9 .... there are millions of cars on the roads. When I was a child, there were far fewer.

10 I promise I won't shout again. .... I'll try to be calm and patient.

11 Ah, you're here .... You must have had a difficult journey.

33 Everyday objects

A Put the letters in order to find the words for the things in Mel's bag.

1 i t e r g h l ....
2 y e k s ....
3 b r l a l m u e ....
4 r i a d y ....
5 a n i t r ....
   m i t e b l e t a ....
6 s o o e l   h g c a e n ....
7 l p s t r e a s ....
8 h b r u s ....
9 s s a g l s e ....
10 s r o s c i s s ....
11 s e u t i s s ....

B Complete the sentences with the words from A.

1 Mel's got a .... to write down all the things she has to do each day.
2 She's got a .... to look up the times of her train.
3 She's got a .... to light her cigarettes.
4 She's got .... to put in the ticket machine at the station.
5 She's got .... in case she cuts herself.
6 She's got .... in case she needs to blow her nose.
7 She's got a small .... in case it rains.
8 She's got her .... so that she can read more easily.
9 She's got a .... so that she can keep her hair tidy.
10 She's got the .... for her flat.
11 She's got .... to cut her fingernails.

34 Household objects and tools

A Complete the sentences with the words in the box.

ashtray   coat hanger   light bulb   tape measure   torch   vase

1 Then all the lights went out and I had to try to find my ....
2 What beautiful flowers, thanks! Let me find a .... to put them in.
3 Have you got a .... I can hang my jacket on?
4 I don't think you can smoke in here. I can't see an .... anywhere.
5 The lamp in the living room isn't working. Where did I put that .... I bought the other day?
6 Get the .... , so we can see how wide the window is.

B Look at the pictures. Write the words from the box in the word web.

drill   hammer   saw   screwdriver

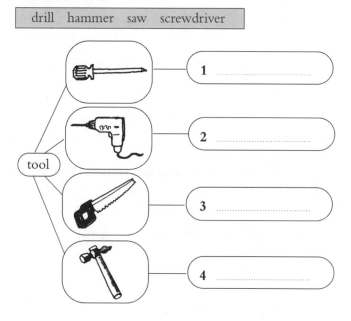

tool

1 ....

2 ....

3 ....

4 ....

35 How good/bad something is

A Find fifteen words in the grid for describing how good or bad something is. Then put the words into the correct group.

e	n	t	e	r	t	a	i	n	i	n	g	d
n	s	w	r	t	e	r	r	i	b	l	e	i
j	f	o	y	n	b	i	u	b	r	e	f	s
o	h	n	u	a	e	n	g	r	e	a	t	a
y	k	d	p	i	r	a	n	i	l	c	n	p
a	v	e	o	a	w	f	u	l	c	a	b	p
b	d	r	e	a	d	f	u	l	s	m	o	o
l	p	f	n	m	u	h	g	i	z	u	r	i
e	y	u	l	y	l	n	c	a	j	s	i	n
g	r	l	d	h	l	m	k	n	g	i	n	t
h	i	n	t	e	r	e	s	t	i	n	g	i
j	w	z	e	x	c	i	t	i	n	g	z	n
k	v	f	a	s	c	i	n	a	t	i	n	g

good: .... , ... , ...

.... , ... , ...

.... , ...

bad: .... , ... , ...

.... , ...

B The <u>underlined</u> words are in the wrong sentences. Write the correct word for each sentence.

1 Her speech was so <u>interesting</u> I almost fell asleep. ....

2 I thought lots of people would be there, but hardly anyone came. It was very <u>amusing</u>. ....

3 It's a very <u>disappointing</u> book. You can learn a lot from it. ....

4 The film was really <u>exciting</u>. I laughed a lot. ....

5 First we missed our flight and then two days after we arrived I broke my leg! It was a <u>boring</u> holiday. ....

6 Riding down the hill was so <u>terrible</u>. I've never been that fast on my bike before. ....

36 Describing objects

A Complete the sentences with the words in the box. Then join the objects with the sentences.

made of   stuff   thing   use for   use to

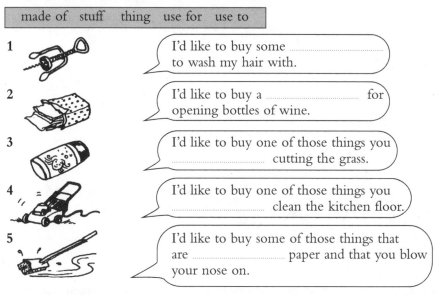

1   I'd like to buy some .... to wash my hair with.

2   I'd like to buy a .... for opening bottles of wine.

3   I'd like to buy one of those things you .... cutting the grass.

4   I'd like to buy one of those things you .... clean the kitchen floor.

5   I'd like to buy some of those things that are .... paper and that you blow your nose on.

B What are the objects made of? Match the words in the box with the groups of objects.

cardboard   glass   leather   material   ~~metal~~
paper   plastic   rubber   wood

1   ....*metal*.......
a car
a knife
scissors

2   ....
a letter
an envelope
a magazine

3   ....
a dress
a towel
curtains

4   ....
a birthday card
a box for chocolates
a book cover

5   ....
a comb
a computer keyboard
a baby's bottle

6   ....
a table
a baseball bat
a fence

7   ....
a window
a light bulb
a beer bottle

8   ....
a wallet
a handbag
a belt

9   ....
a tyre
gloves for washing up
a ball

37 Using your eyes

A Circle the correct word in each pair.

1
gaze / wink

2
examine / glance

3
frown / look at

4
blink / peep

5
look for / stare

6
glare / squint

B Complete the sentences with the other words from A.
Remember to put the verbs in the correct form.

1 Don't .... at people. It's not very polite.

2 She quickly .... around the room to see if she knew anyone there.

3 He blew on her face, making her ....

4 He sat .... out of the window, thinking about when he might see her again.

5 She .... at him. She was so angry about what he had done.

6 Here, ... this photograph – it's me when I was five years old.

A Find the words for ten ways of walking in the grid. Then complete the words in the list.

p	a	d	d	l	e	c	q	e	n
b	n	o	m	i	j	r	p	s	j
d	e	s	k	i	p	a	w	l	v
g	r	t	s	z	g	w	l	i	h
l	h	c	l	i	k	l	c	p	n
i	k	b	c	b	h	m	e	i	n
m	m	a	r	c	h	t	h	o	p
p	q	a	e	s	t	r	o	l	l
i	s	w	e	u	f	i	m	k	h
l	t	v	p	f	l	p	y	r	t

1 cra ....
2 cre ....
3 h ....
4 l ....
5 m ....
6 p ....
7 sk ....
8 sl ....
9 st ....
10 t ....

B Label the pictures with five of the words from A.

1

....

2

....

3

....

4

....

5

....

C Match the definitions with the other five words from A.

1 to walk somewhere in a slow, relaxed way ....

2 to walk very quietly and carefully ....

3 to move about by jumping up and down on one foot ....

4 to walk with difficulty because one of your legs or feet is hurt ....

5 to move forwards by jumping quickly on one foot then the other and lifting your knees high ....

39 Phrasal verbs

A Match the words in the box with the pictures.

Calm down!   Cheer up!   Come on!
Hang on!   Slow down!   Speed up!

B Complete the sentences with the words in the box.

make   pick   put   take

1 If you don't like the situation, don't just .... up with it.
  Do something to change it.

2 My train gets in at 17.30. Will you be able to .... me up
  or should I get a taxi to your house?

3 Don't believe everything they tell you. They .... up
  stories all the time.

4 I want something to do in my spare time, so I've decided to
  .... up golf.

40 Giving your opinion

A Put the expressions in the box into three groups.

as far as I'm concerned   I believe in   I have my doubts about
I'm against   I'm in favour of   in my opinion
in my view   to my mind

expressing your opinion

....

....

positive opinion   **negative opinion**

....

....

B Read the sentences. Then rewrite them with the other four expressions from A.

1 In my opinion, parking charges should be higher.

As ....

2 In my view, there should be more cycle tracks.

To ....

3 I have my doubts about reducing bus fares.

....

4 I believe in increasing speed limits on motorways.

....

C Complete the conversations with the words in the box.

about   agree   disagree   of   think   view

Jane: What do you think (1) .... his latest film?
Lawrence: I (2) .... it's really great.
Holly: Oh no, I (3) .... The one he made last year
            was much better.

Steven: What do you think (4) .... moving to a
            different office?
Millie: Well, it's only my point of (5) .... , but I'd
            prefer to stay here.
Vivien: Yes, I (6) .... I'd rather stay here too.

Test 4 (Units 31-40)

A Complete the sentences.

1 The words 'tree', 'computer' and 'enemy' are all ....

2 The words 'feel', 'fry' and 'arrest' are all ....

3 The words 'arrogant', 'romantic' and 'delicious' are all ....

4 The words 'quickly', 'slowly' and 'happily' are all ....

B Write another time expression which means the same.

1 for a very long time ....

2 not very often ....

3 not early and not late ....

4 not any more ....

5 up till now ....

6 right now ....

C Complete the sentences to describe the objects.

1   2   3   4

1 This .... is made of .... and you
.... it .... hold flowers.

2 These .... are made of .... and you
.... them .... blow your nose.

3 These .... are made of .... and you
.... them .... cutting things.

4 This .... is made of .... and you
.... it .... finding out how big something is.

D Put the words in the box in three groups.

awful boring brilliant disappointing dreadful dull great terrible wonderful

very bad   **very good**   **not interesting**

....

....

....

Test 4 (Units 31–40)

E The <u>underlined</u> words are in the wrong sentences. Write the correct word for each sentence.

1 He's <u>limping</u> because the sun's in his eyes. ....

2 She's <u>peeping</u> in the water. ....

3 He's <u>creeping</u> through the hole to see what's there. ....

4 He's <u>paddling</u> up the stairs because he doesn't want anyone to hear him. ....

5 She's <u>blinking</u> because she's confused. ....

6 He's <u>frowning</u> because he's hurt his leg. ....

F Write a phrasal verb for each definition.

1 become happy after being sad ....

2 wait ....

3 collect ....

4 go slower ....

5 start doing a sport or hobby ....

6 go faster ....

G Put the words in order to make sentences.

1 far it's right not as I'm as concerned

....

2 think you what about do it?

....

3 favour in it of I'm

....

4 my in it's wrong opinion

....

5 it against I'm

....

Answer Key

1 Family

A
1 kids
2 only child
3 partner
4 ex-wife
5 orphan
6 twins
7 triplets
8 ex-husband

2 People's ages

A
1 *Buy the learn-to-write game for Anne-Sophie – she's a child.*
2 Buy the rattle for Gianni – he's a baby.
3 Buy the tricycle for Melanie – she's a toddler.
4 Buy the trainers for Nicola – she's a teenager.
5 Buy the theatre tickets for Gary – he's an adult.

B
1 *death*
2 teens
3 late
4 middle-aged
5 birth
6 twenties
7 childhood
8 early
9 old age

3 Describing character 1

A
1 *Maxine*
2 Simon
3 Jerry
4 Dominic
5 Jake
6 Lily
7 Maxine
8 Jerry
9 Dominic
10 Simon
11 Jake
12 Lily

4 Describing character 2

A
1 immature
2 creative
3 charming
4 reasonable
5 mature
6 modest

B
1 sociable
2 loyal
3 sensitive
4 optimistic
5 pessimistic
6 vain

5 How you feel

A
1 confused
2 nervous
3 depressed
4 shocked
5 excited
6 upset

B
1 stressed
2 frustrated
3 homesick
4 relieved
5 disappointed
6 satisfied

6 Love and marriage

A
1 divorced
2 single
3 separated
4 married
5 widowed

B
1 fancied
2 going out with
3 relationship
4 an affair
5 split up
6 living with
7 romantic

7 Your body

A 1 *spine*
2 muscle
3 eyebrow
4 palm

5 skin
6 eyelashes
7 bone
8 eyelid

9 lungs
10 brain
11 ribs
12 heart

B 1 palm
2 muscle
3 eyelid
4 skin
5 spine
6 bone

8 The senses

A 1 a sound
2 a noise
3 listen
4 hear

5 a sight
6 see
7 look
8 watch

B 1 smell
2 touch
3 Feel
4 taste
5 feels

6 Taste
7 tastes
8 smells
9 smell

9 Driving a car

A 1 clutch
2 ignition
3 brake
4 driving
licence
5 accelerator
6 driving test

B 1 in neutral
2 start up
3 in first gear
4 move off
5 Speed up
6 change gear

7 overtake
8 indicate
9 slow down
10 park
11 reverse

10 Signs

A 1 out of order
2 do not
disturb
3 for sale
4 to let

5 on time
6 delayed
7 nothing to
declare
8 reserved

9 no entry
10 do not bend
11 fragile
12 sale

Test 1 (Units 1–10)

A 1 twins, our
late thirties
2 divorced
3 ex-husband
4 partner,
his forties

B **Mike**
intelligent,
arrogant
Heather easy-
going, vain
Jack creative,
pessimistic

C 1 stressed
2 homesick
3 frustrated
4 excited

D 1 eyebrow
2 eyelid
3 eyelashes
4 bone
5 muscle

E 1 hearing
2 watch
3 noise
4 see

F 1 parking
2 overtaking
3 reversing
4 indicating

G 1 out of order
2 on time
3 sale
4 reserved

11 Television

A 1 cartoon
2 the news
3 soap opera
4 documentary
5 chat show
6 game show

B 1 Now, what shall I watch tonight?
2 I'll be back tomorrow with the nine o'clock news, so until then, goodnight.
3 Tonight we are going to look at crime in our cities and what's being done about it.
4 My first guest tonight is the actor and singer, Joel Williams.

12 Cinema

A 1 science fiction film
2 thriller
3 war film
4 horror film
5 western
6 action film
7 animated film
8 comedy

B 1 film star
2 make-up artist
3 actress
4 actor
5 cameraman
6 costume designer
7 director
8 producer

13 Newspapers and magazines

A 1 *a daily*
2 a local newspaper
3 a broadsheet
4 a weekly
5 a national newspaper
6 a tabloid

B 1 She's an editor.
2 He's a reporter.
3 He's a member of the paparazzi.

C 1 headline
2 article
3 the press
4 feature

14 Books

A 1 guidebook
2 dictionary
3 cookery book
4 atlas
5 encyclopedia
6 textbook
7 biography
8 computer manual
9 comic
10 novel
11 autobiography

B 1 hardback
2 character
3 chapter
4 title
5 paperback
6 author

15 Cooking

A 1 fried
2 roasted
3 boiled
4 baked
5 grilled

B 1 Chop
2 Grate
3 Squeeze
4 Slice
5 Spread
6 Peel

16 The taste of food

A 1 spicy
2 bitter
3 sweet
4 sour

B 1 e
2 d
3 a
4 f
5 b
6 c

17 Sounds

A 1 buzz
2 splash
3 crunch
4 pop
5 ring
6 sizzle
7 bang
8 fizz
9 creak
10 crackle

B 1 buzzing
2 splashing
3 crunches
4 popped
5 Ring
6 sizzle
7 banging
8 fizzing
9 creaks
10 crackles

18 Home technology

A 1 burglar alarm
2 CD player
3 cordless phone
4 digital camera
5 DVD player
6 minidisc player
7 radio-alarm clock
8 remote control
9 satellite dish
10 widescreen TV

B 1 minidisc player
2 widescreen TV
3 CD player
4 DVD player
5 satellite dish
6 digital camera
7 cordless phone
8 remote control
9 burglar alarm
10 radio-alarm clock

C 1 cordless phone
2 widescreen TV
3 minidisc player
4 radio-alarm clock
5 digital camera
6 remote control

19 The environment

A 1 ozone layer
2 global warming
3 greenhouse effect
4 nuclear waste
5 exhaust fumes
6 acid rain

B 1 nuclear waste
2 exhaust fumes
3 ozone layer
4 acid rain
5 greenhouse effect
6 global warming

C 1 polluting
2 pollution
3 organic
4 pesticides
5 Recycle
6 recycling

20 Natural disasters

A 1 flood
2 earthquake
3 forest fire
4 hurricane
5 volcanic eruption
6 drought
7 avalanche

B 1 death toll
2 victims
3 state of emergency
4 rescue operation
5 Rescue workers
6 casualties
7 survivors

Test 2 (Units 11–20)

A
1 chat show
2 comedy
3 game show
4 western
5 horror film
6 documentary

B
1 tabloid
2 novel
3 local newspaper
4 atlas

C
1 Peel, chop, fry
2 squeeze, roast
3 boil, grate

D
1 bitter
2 sweet
3 spicy
4 mild
5 rich
6 salty

E
1 banged
2 sizzled
3 splash
4 creaked
5 pop

F
1 remote control
2 burglar alarm
3 satellite dish
4 radio-alarm clock

G
1 rescue workers
2 hurricane
3 pollution
4 recycling
5 organic
6 survivors

21 Studying at university

A
1 law
2 medicine
3 politics
4 business studies
5 agriculture
6 architecture
7 engineering
8 modern languages
9 journalism

B
1 student
2 lecturer
3 degree
4 lecture
5 seminar

22 Crime

A
1 b
2 a
3 d
4 c

B
1 shoplifter
2 murderer
3 terrorist
4 burglar

C
1 burglary
2 arrested
3 broke into
4 steal
5 criminals
6 committing
7 victims

23 Law and justice

A
1 judge
2 court
3 jury
4 lawyer

B
1 c
2 d
3 b
4 h
5 a
6 e
7 g
8 f

24 Getting a job

A
1 interview
2 Salary
3 pension
4 application form
5 benefits
6 advertisement
7 qualifications
8 reference
9 apply
10 vacancy
11 experience
12 CV

B
1 vacancy
2 experience
3 application form
4 salary
5 qualifications
6 benefits
7 Interviews

25 Talking about your work

A 1 do
2 as
3 for
4 in

B 1 employed
2 earning
3 training
4 long hours
5 from home

6 the office
7 promoted
8 pay rise
9 set up
10 unemployed

11 made redundant
12 temporary
13 permanent

26 Who works in a company

A 1 sales manager
2 personnel manager
3 sales representative, boss
4 accounts manager

5 chief executive, managing director
6 receptionist
7 personal assistant
8 secretary

27 Money

A 1 *bills*
2 wages
3 mortgage
4 rent
5 interest
6 taxes

B 1 taxes
2 mortgage
3 rent
4 bills
5 wages
6 interest

C 1 loss
2 poor
3 owe
4 expenses
5 profit
6 afford
7 rich

28 Using a computer

A 1 delete
2 open
3 close
4 edit
5 exit

6 save
7 copy
8 paste
9 cut
10 print

B 1 open
2 copy
3 print
4 save

C 1 Highlight
2 Scroll
3 Click
4 key

29 Politics

A 1 politicians
2 government
3 president / prime minister
4 ministers

B 1 holding an election
2 vote for
3 candidates
4 elected
5 policies
6 political party
7 be in power

30 War and peace

A 1 army
2 enemy
3 ally
4 prisoners
5 civilians

B 1 invaded
2 attacked
3 captured
4 defend
5 retreat

6 declared
7 ceasefire
8 peace talks

Test 3 (Units 21–30)

A 1 medicine
2 agriculture
3 engineering
4 journalism
5 modern languages
6 law

B 1 c
2 f
3 d
4 b
5 e
6 a

C 1 work for
2 sales manager
3 sales representative
4 promoted
5 unemployed
6 you do

D 1 applied for
2 advertisement
3 CV
4 interview
5 salary
6 mortgage

E 1 copy
2 highlight
3 paste
4 scroll
5 print
6 save
7 delete
8 edit
9 cut
10 exit

F 1 politician
2 prisoner
3 candidate
4 civilian
5 minister

31 Talking about language

A 1 grammar
2 adverbs
3 translate
4 accent
5 informal
6 vocabulary
7 Nouns
8 adjectives
9 Pronunciation
10 formal
11 verb

B 1 How do you spell 'sociable'?
2 What does 'muscle' mean?
3 How do you pronounce 'squeeze'?

32 Expressions of time

A 1 for
2 now
3 these
4 so
5 at
6 no
7 from
8 at
9 at
10 in
11 on

B 1 now and then
2 at once
3 in time
4 on time
5 at the moment
6 no longer
7 for ages
8 so far
9 These days
10 From now on
11 at last

33 Everyday objects

A 1 lighter
2 keys
3 umbrella
4 diary
5 train timetable
6 loose change
7 plasters
8 brush
9 glasses
10 scissors
11 tissues

B 1 diary
2 train timetable
3 lighter
4 loose change
5 plasters
6 tissues
7 umbrella
8 glasses
9 brush
10 keys
11 scissors

34 Household objects and tools

A
1 torch
2 vase
3 coat hanger
4 ashtray
5 light bulb
6 tape measure

B
1 screwdriver
2 drill
3 saw
4 hammer

35 How good/bad something is

A

good	bad
amusing	awful
brilliant	boring
enjoyable	disappointing
entertaining	dreadful
exciting	dull
fascinating	terrible
great	
interesting	
wonderful	

B
1 boring
2 disappointing
3 interesting
4 amusing
5 terrible
6 exciting

36 Describing objects

A
1 thing
2 made of
3 stuff
4 use for
5 use to

B
1 *metal*
2 paper
3 material
4 cardboard
5 plastic
6 wood
7 glass
8 leather
9 rubber

37 Using your eyes

A
1 wink
2 examine
3 frown
4 peep
5 look for
6 squint

B
1 stare
2 glanced
3 blink
4 gazing
5 glared
6 look at

38 Ways of walking

A
1 crawl
2 creep
3 hop
4 limp
5 march
6 paddle
7 skip
8 slip
9 stroll
10 trip

B
1 march
2 crawl
3 slip
4 paddle
5 trip

C
1 stroll
2 creep
3 hop
4 limp
5 skip

39 Phrasal verbs

A 1 Cheer up!　　**B** 1 put
2 Slow down!　　　 2 pick
3 Come on!　　　　 3 make
4 Speed up!　　　　 4 take
5 Calm down!
6 Hang on!

40 Giving your opinion

A **expressing your opinion**
as far as I'm concerned
in my opinion
in my view
to my mind
positive opinion
I believe in
I'm in favour of
negative opinion
I have my doubts about
I'm against

B 1 As far as I'm concerned, parking charges should be higher.
2 To my mind, there should be more cycle tracks.
3 I'm against reducing bus fares.
4 I'm in favour of increasing speed limits on motorways.

C 1 of
2 think
3 disagree
4 about
5 view
6 agree

Test 4 (Units 31–40)

A 1 nouns
2 verbs
3 adjectives
4 adverbs

B 1 for ages
2 now and then
3 on time
4 no longer
5 so far
6 at once

C 1 vase, glass, use, to
2 tissues, paper, use, to
3 scissors, metal, use, for
4 tape measure, plastic, use, for

D **very bad**
awful, dreadful, terrible
very good
brilliant, great, wonderful
not interesting
boring, disappointing, dull

E 1 blinking
2 paddling
3 peeping
4 creeping
5 frowning
6 limping

F 1 cheer up
2 hang on
3 pick up
4 slow down
5 take up
6 speed up

G 1 As far as I'm concerned, it's not right.
2 What do you think about it?
3 I'm in favour of it.
4 In my opinion, it's wrong.
5 I'm against it.

Word List

The words in this list are British English. Sometimes we give you an important American English word which means the same.

1 Family
ex-husband /ˌeks hʌzbənd/
ex-wife /ˌeks'waɪf/
kids /kɪdz/ (informal)
only child /ˌəʊnli 'tʃaɪld/
orphan /'ɔːfən/
partner /'pɑːtnə/
triplets /'trɪpləts/
twins /twɪnz/

2 People's ages
adult /'ædʌlt/
baby /'beɪbi/
birth /bɜːθ/
child /tʃaɪld/ (plural = children)
childhood /'tʃaɪldhʊd/
death /deθ/
in your teens /ɪn jɔː 'tiːnz/
in your twenties /ɪn jɔː 'twentiz/
late twenties /ˌleɪt 'twentiz/
early thirties /ˌɜːli 'θɜːtiz/
middle-aged /ˌmɪdl'eɪdʒd/
old age /ˌəʊld 'eɪdʒ/
teenager /'tiːnˌeɪdʒə/
toddler /'tɒdlə/

3 Describing character 1
ambitious /æm'bɪʃəs/
arrogant /'ærəgənt/
confident /'kɒnfɪdənt/
easy-going /ˌiːzi'gəʊɪŋ/
hard-working /ˌhɑːd'wɜːkɪŋ/
have a good sense of humour /hæv ə ˌgʊd ˌsens əv 'hjuːmə/

independent /ˌɪndɪˈpendənt/
intelligent /ɪnˈtelɪdʒənt/
organized /ˈɔːgənaɪzd/
quiet /kwaɪət/
romantic /rəˈmæntɪk/
serious /ˈsɪəriəs/

4 Describing character 2

charming /ˈtʃɑːmɪŋ/
creative /kriˈeɪtɪv/
immature /ˌɪməˈtjʊə/
loyal /lɔɪəl/
mature /məˈtjʊə/
modest /ˈmɒdɪst/
optimistic /ˌɒptɪˈmɪstɪk/
pessimistic /ˌpesɪˈmɪstɪk/
reasonable /ˈriːzənəbl/
sensitive /ˈsensɪtɪv/
sociable /ˈsəʊʃəbl/
vain /veɪn/

5 How you feel

confused /kənˈfjuːzd/
depressed /dɪˈprest/
disappointed /ˌdɪsəˈpɔɪntɪd/
excited /ɪkˈsaɪtɪd/
frustrated /frʌsˈtreɪtɪd/
homesick /ˈhəʊmsɪk/
nervous /ˈnɜːvəs/
relieved /rɪˈliːvd/
satisfied /ˈsætɪsfaɪd/
shocked /ʃɒkt/
stressed /strest/
upset /ʌpˈset/

6 Love and marriage

affair /əˈfeə/
divorced /dɪˈvɔːst/
fancy /ˈfænsi/ (informal)
go out with /ˌɡəʊ ˈaʊt wɪð/ (*past tense* went, *past participle* gone)
live with /ˈlɪv wɪð/
married /ˈmærid/
relationship /rɪˈleɪʃənʃɪp/
romantic /rəˈmæntɪk/
separated /ˈsepəreɪtɪd/
single /ˈsɪŋɡl/
split up /ˌsplɪt ˈʌp/ (*past tense* & *past participle* split)
widowed /ˈwɪdəʊd/

7 Your body

bone /bəʊn/
brain /breɪn/
eyebrow /ˈaɪbraʊ/
eyelashes /ˈaɪlæʃɪz/
eyelid /ˈaɪlɪd/
heart /hɑːt/
lungs /lʌŋz/
muscle /ˈmʌsl/
palm /pɑːm/
ribs /rɪbz/
skin /skɪn/
spine /spaɪn/

8 The senses

feel /fiːl/ (*past tense* & *past participle* felt)
hear /hɪə/ (*past tense* & *past participle* heard)
hearing /ˈhɪərɪŋ/
listen /ˈlɪsən/
look /lʊk/
noise /nɔɪz/
see /siː/ (*past tense* saw, *past participle* seen)
sight /saɪt/
smell /smel/ (*past tense* & *past participle* smelt *or* smelled)

sound /saʊnd/
taste /teɪst/
touch /tʌtʃ/
watch /wɒtʃ/

9 Driving a car

accelerator /əkˈseləreɪtə/
brake (noun) /breɪk/
change gear /ˌtʃeɪndʒ ˈgɪə/
clutch /klʌtʃ/
driving licence /ˈdraɪvɪŋ ˌlaɪsəns/
driving test /ˈdraɪvɪŋ ˌtest/
ignition /ɪgˈnɪʃən/
indicate /ˈɪndɪkeɪt/
in first gear /ɪn ˌfɜːst ˈgɪə/
in neutral /ɪn ˈnjuːtrəl/
move off /ˌmuːv ˈɒf/
overtake /ˌəʊvəˈteɪk/
park /pɑːk/
reverse /rɪˈvɜːs/
slow down /ˌsləʊ ˈdaʊn/
speed up /ˌspiːd ˈʌp/
start up /ˌstɑːt ˈʌp/

10 Signs

delayed /dɪˈleɪd/
do not bend /ˌduː nɒt ˈbend/
do not disturb /ˌduː nɒt dɪˈstɜːb/
for sale /fə ˈseɪl/
fragile /ˈfrædʒaɪl/
no entry /ˌnəʊ ˈentri/
nothing to declare /ˌnʌθɪŋ tə dɪˈkleə/
on time /ˌɒn taɪm/
out of order /ˌaʊt əv ˈɔːdə/
reserved /rɪˈzɜːvd/
sale /seɪl/
to let /tə ˈlet/

11 Television

cartoon /kɑːˈtuːn/
chat show /ˈtʃæt ˌʃəʊ/ (US = talk show)
chat show host /ˈtʃæt ˌʃəʊ ˌhəʊst/
documentary /ˌdɒkjəˈmentəri/
game show /ˈɡeɪm ˌʃəʊ/
newsreader /ˈnjuːzˌriːdə/ (US = newscaster)
presenter /prɪˈzentə/
the news /ðə ˈnjuːz/
soap opera /ˈsəʊpˌɒpərə/
viewer /ˈvjuːə/

12 Cinema

action film /ˈækʃən fɪlm/
actor /ˈæktə/ (can be used for a man or a woman)
actress /ˈæktrəs/ (some women prefer to be called *actor*)
animated film /ˌænɪmeɪtɪd ˈfɪlm/
cameraman /ˈkæmərəmæn/
comedy /ˈkɒmədi/
costume designer /ˈkɒstjuːm dɪˌzaɪnə/
director /dɪˈrektə/
film star /ˈfɪlm ˌstɑː/
horror film /ˈhɒrə ˌfɪlm/
make-up artist /ˈmeɪkʌp ˌɑːtɪst/
producer /prəˈdjuːsə/
science fiction film /ˌsaɪəns ˈfɪkʃən ˌfɪlm/
thriller /ˈθrɪlə/
war film /ˈwɔː ˌfɪlm/
western /ˈwestən/

13 Newspapers and magazines

article /ˈɑːtɪkl/
broadsheet /ˈbrɔːdʃiːt/
daily /ˈdeɪli/
editor /ˈedɪtə/
feature /ˈfiːtʃə/
headline /ˈhedlaɪn/
local newspaper /ˌləʊkəl ˈnjuːsˌpeɪpə/

national newspaper /ˌnæʃənəl 'njuːsˌpeɪpə/
paparazzi /ˌpæpər'ætsi/
the press /ðə 'pres/
reporter /rɪ'pɔːtə/
tabloid /'tæblɔɪd/
weekly /'wiːkli/

14 Books
atlas /'ætləs/
author /'ɔːθə/
autobiography /ˌɔːtəbaɪ'ɒgrəfi/
biography /baɪ'ɒgrəfi/
chapter /'tʃæptə/
character /'kærəktə/
comic /'kɒmɪk/
computer manual /kəm'pjuːtə ˌmænjuəl/
cookery book /'kʊkəri ˌbʊk/
dictionary /'dɪkʃənəri/
encyclopedia /ɪnˌsaɪklə'piːdiə/
guidebook /'gaɪdbʊk/
hardback /'hɑːdbæk/
novel /'nɒvəl/
paperback /'peɪpəbæk/
textbook /'teksbʊk/
title /'taɪtl/

15 Cooking
bake /beɪk/
boil /bɔɪl/
chop /tʃɒp/
fry /fraɪ/
grate /greɪt/
grill /grɪl/
peel /piːl/
roast /rəʊst/
slice /slaɪs/
spread /spred/ (*past tense* & *past participle* spread)
squeeze /skwiːz/

16 The taste of food

bitter /ˈbɪtə/
delicious /dɪˈlɪʃəs/
horrible /ˈhɒrəbl/
mild /maɪld/
rich /rɪtʃ/
salty /ˈsɔːlti/
sour /saʊə/
spicy /ˈspaɪsi/
sweet /swiːt/
tasteless /ˈteɪsləs/

17 Sounds

bang /bæŋ/
buzz /bʌz/
crackle /ˈkrækl/
creak /kriːk/
crunch /krʌnʃ/
fizz /fɪz/
pop /pɒp/
ring /rɪŋ/ (*past tense* rang, *past participle* rung)
sizzle /ˈsɪzl/
splash /splæʃ/

18 Home technology

burglar alarm /ˈbɜːglə əˌlɑːm/
CD player /ˌsiːˈdiː ˌpleɪə/
cordless phone /ˌkɔːdləs ˈfəʊn/
digital camera /ˌdɪdʒɪtəl ˈkæmərə/
DVD player /ˌdiːviːˈdiː ˌpleɪə/
minidisc player /ˈmɪnidɪsk ˌpleɪə/
radio-alarm clock /ˌreɪdiəʊ əˈlɑːm ˌklɒk/
remote control /rɪˌməʊt kənˈtrəʊl/
satellite dish /ˈsætəlaɪt ˌdɪʃ/
widescreen TV /ˌwaɪdskriːn ˌtiːˈviː/

19 The environment
acid rain /ˌæsɪd 'reɪn/
exhaust fumes /ɪg'zɔːst ˌfjuːmz/
global warming /ˌgləʊbəl 'wɔːmɪŋ/
greenhouse effect /'griːnhaʊs ɪˌfekt/
nuclear waste /ˌnjuːkliə 'weɪst/
organic /ɔː'gænɪk/
ozone layer /'əʊzəʊn ˌleɪə/
pesticides /'pestɪsaɪdz/
pollute /pə'luːt/
pollution /pə'luːʃən/
recycle /ˌriː'saɪkl/
recycling /ˌriː'saɪklɪŋ/

20 Natural disasters
avalanche /'ævəlɑːnʃ/
casualties /'kæʒjuəltiz/
death toll /'deθ ˌtəʊl/
drought /draʊt/
earthquake /'ɜːθkweɪk/
flood /flʌd/
forest fire /ˌfɒrɪst 'faɪə/
hurricane /'hʌrɪkən/
rescue operation /'reskjuː ˌɒpərˌeɪʃən/
rescue workers /'reskjuː ˌwɜːkəz/
state of emergency /ˌsteɪt əv ɪ'mɜːdʒənsi/
survivors /sə'vaɪvəz/
victims /'vɪktɪmz/
volcanic eruption /vɒlˌkænɪk ɪ'rʌpʃən/

21 Studying at university
agriculture /'ægrɪkʌltʃə/
architecture /'ɑːkɪtektʃə/
business studies /'bɪznɪs ˌstʌdiz/
degree /dɪ'griː/
engineering /ˌendʒɪ'nɪərɪŋ/
journalism /'dʒɜːnəlɪzəm/
law /lɔː/

lecture /'lektʃə/
lecturer /'lektʃərə/ (US = teacher or professor)
medicine /'medsən/
modern languages /ˌmɒdən 'læŋgwɪdʒɪz/
politics /'pɒlətɪks/
seminar /'semɪnɑː/
student /'stjuːdənt/

22 Crime

arrest /ə'rest/
break into /ˌbreɪk 'ɪntə/ (*past tense* broke, *past participle* broken)
burglar /'bɜːglə/
burglary /'bɜːgləri/
commit a crime /kəˌmɪt ə 'kraɪm/
criminal /'krɪmɪnəl/
murder /'mɜːdə/
murderer /'mɜːdərə/
shoplifter /'ʃɒpˌlɪftə/
shoplifting /'ʃɒplɪftɪŋ/
steal /stiːl/ (*past tense* stole, *past participle* stolen)
terrorism /'terərɪzəm/
terrorist /'terərɪst/
victim /'vɪktɪm/

23 Law and justice

court /kɔːt/
evidence /'evɪdəns/
guilty /'gɪlti/
innocent /'ɪnəsənt/
judge /dʒʌdʒ/
jury /'dʒʊəri/
lawyer /'lɔɪə/ (US = attorney)
police /pə'liːs/
prison /'prɪzən/
sentence /'sentəns/
witness /'wɪtnəs/

24 Getting a job

advertisement /əd'vɜːtɪsmənt/
application form /ˌæplɪ'keɪʃən ˌfɔːm/
apply /ə'plaɪ/
benefits /'benɪfɪts/
CV /ˌsiː'viː/ (curriculum vitae) (US = résumé)
experience /ɪk'spɪəriəns/
interview /'ɪntəvjuː/
pension /'penʃən/
qualifications /ˌkwɒlɪfɪ'keɪʃənz/
reference /'refərəns/
salary /'sæləri/
vacancy /'veɪkənsi/

25 Talking about your work

be made redundant /biː ˌmeɪd rɪ'dʌndənt/
be promoted /ˌbiː prə'məʊtɪd/
earning /'ɜːnɪŋ/
employed /ɪm'plɔɪd/
pay rise /'peɪ ˌraɪz/
permanent /'pɜːmənənt/
set up a business /ˌset ʌp ə 'bɪznɪs/ (past tense & past participle set)
temporary /'tempərəri/
the office /ði: 'ɒfɪs/
training /'treɪnɪŋ/
unemployed /ˌʌnɪm'plɔɪd/
what do you do? /ˌwɒt duː juː 'duː/
work as /'wɜːk əz/
work for /'wɜːk fɔː/
work from home /ˌwɜːk frəm 'həʊm/
work in /'wɜːk ɪn/
work long hours /ˌwɜːk ˌlɒŋ 'aʊəz/

26 Who works in a company
accounts manager /əˈkaʊnts ˌmænɪdʒə/
boss /bɒs/
chief executive /ˌtʃiːf ɪgˈzekjətɪv/
managing director /ˌmænɪdʒɪŋ daɪˈrektə/
personal assistant /ˌpɜːsənəl əˈsɪstənt/
personnel manager /ˌpɜːsənˈel ˌmænɪdʒə/
receptionist /rɪˈsepʃənɪst/
sales manager /ˈseɪlz ˌmænɪdʒə/
sales representative /seɪlz ˌreprɪˌzentətɪv/
secretary /ˈsekrətəri/

27 Money
afford /əˈfɔːd/
bills /bɪlz/
expenses /ɪkˈspensɪz/
interest /ˈɪntrəst/
loss /lɒs/
mortgage /ˈmɔːgɪdʒ/
owe /əʊ/
poor /pɔː/
profit /ˈprɒfɪt/
rent /rent/
rich /rɪtʃ/
taxes /ˈtæksɪz/
wages /ˈweɪdʒɪz/

28 Using a computer
click on /ˌklɪk ˈɒn/
close /kləʊz/
copy /ˈkɒpi/
cut /kʌt/ (*past tense & past participle* cut)
delete /dɪˈliːt/
edit /ˈedɪt/
exit /ˈeksɪt/
highlight /ˈhaɪlaɪt/
key /kiː/

open /'əupən/
paste /peɪst/
print /prɪnt/
save /seɪv/
scroll /skrəul/

29 Politics

be elected /biː ɪˈlektɪd/
be in power /biː ɪn ˈpauə/
candidate /ˈkændɪdət/
government /ˈgʌvənmənt/
hold an election /ˌhəuld ən ɪˈlekʃən/ (*past tense & past participle* held)
minister /ˈmɪnɪstə/
policy /ˈpɒləsi/
political party /pəˌlɪtɪkəl ˈpɑːti/
politician /ˌpɒlɪˈtɪʃən/
president /ˈprezɪdənt/
prime minister /ˌpraɪm ˈmɪnɪstə/
vote for /ˈvəut ˌfɔː/

30 War and peace

ally /ˈælaɪ/
army /ˈɑːmi/
attack /əˈtæk/
capture /ˈkæptʃə/
ceasefire /ˈsiːsfaɪə/
civilians /sɪˈvɪliənz/
declare /dɪˈkleə/
defend /dɪˈfend/
enemy /ˈenəmi/
invade /ɪnˈveɪd/
peace talks /ˈpiːs ˌtɔːks/
prisoners /ˈprɪzənəz/
retreat /rɪˈtriːt/

31 Talking about language

accent /'æksənt/
adjective /'ædʒɪktɪv/
adverb /'ædvɜːb/
formal /'fɔːməl/
grammar /'græmə/
informal /ɪn'fɔːməl/
mean /miːn/ (*past tense* & *past participle* meant)
noun /naʊn/
pronounce /prə'naʊns/
pronunciation /prə,nʌnsi'eɪʃən/
spell /spel/ (*past tense* & *past participle* spelt *or* spelled)
translate /trænz'leɪt/
verb /vɜːb/
vocabulary /və'kæbjələri/

32 Expressions of time

at last /ət 'lɑːst/
at once /ət 'wʌns/
at the moment /ət ðə 'məʊmənt/
for ages /fɔːr eɪdʒɪz/
from now on /frəm ,naʊ 'ɒn/
in time /,ɪn 'taɪm/
no longer /,nəʊ 'lɒŋgə/
now and then /,naʊ ən 'ðen/
on time /,ɒn 'taɪm/
so far /,səʊ 'fɑː/
these days /'ðiːz ,deɪz/

33 Everyday objects

brush /brʌʃ/
diary /'daɪəri/
keys /kiːz/
lighter /'laɪtə/
loose change /'luːs 'tʃeɪndʒ/
plasters /'plɑːstəz/

scissors /'sɪzəz/
tissues /'tɪʃuːz/
train timetable /'treɪn ˌtaɪmˌteɪbl/
umbrella /ʌm'brelə/

34 Household objects and tools

ashtray /'æʃˌtreɪ/
coat hanger /'kəʊt ˌhæŋə/
drill /drɪl/
hammer /'hæmə/
light bulb /'laɪt ˌbʌlb/
saw /sɔː/
screwdriver /'skruːˌdraɪvə/
tape measure /'teɪp ˌmeʒə/
tool /tuːl/
torch /tɔːtʃ/ (US = flashlight)
vase /vɑːz/

35 How good/bad something is

amusing /ə'mjuːzɪŋ/
awful /'ɔːfəl/
boring /'bɔːrɪŋ/
brilliant /'brɪliənt/
disappointing /ˌdɪsə'pɔɪntɪŋ/
dreadful /'dredfəl/
dull /dʌl/
enjoyable /ɪn'dʒɔɪəbl/
entertaining /ˌentə'teɪnɪŋ/
exciting /ɪk'saɪtɪŋ/
fascinating /'fæsɪneɪtɪŋ/
great /greɪt/
interesting /'ɪntrəstɪŋ/
terrible /'terəbl/
wonderful /'wʌndəfəl/

36 Describing objects

cardboard /ˈkɑːdbɔːd/
glass /glɑːs/
leather /ˈleðə/
made of /ˈmeɪd ɒv/
material /məˈtɪəriəl/
metal /ˈmetəl/
paper /ˈpeɪpə/
plastic /ˈplæstɪk/
rubber /ˈrʌbə/
stuff /stʌf/
thing /θɪŋ/
use for /ˈjuːs fə/
use to /ˈjuːs tə/
wood /wʊd/

37 Using your eyes

blink /blɪŋk/
examine /ɪgˈzæmɪn/
frown /fraʊn/
gaze /geɪz/
glance /glɑːns/
glare /gleə/
look at /ˈlʊk ət/
look for /ˈlʊk fə/
peep /piːp/
squint /skwɪnt/
stare /steə/
wink /wɪŋk/

38 Ways of walking

crawl /krɔːl/
creep /kriːp/ (*past tense* & *past participle* crept)
hop /hɒp/
limp /lɪmp/
march /mɑːtʃ/

paddle /ˈpædl/
skip /skɪp/
slip /slɪp/
stroll /strəʊl/
trip /trɪp/

39 Phrasal verbs

calm down /ˌkɑːm ˈdaʊn/
cheer up /ˌtʃɪə ˈʌp/
come on /ˌkʌm ˈɒn/ (*past tense* came, *past participle* come)
hang on /ˌhæŋ ˈɒn/ (*past tense* & *past participle* hung)
make up /ˌmeɪk ˈʌp/ (*past tense* & *past participle* made)
pick up /ˌpɪk ˈʌp/
put up with /ˌpʊt ˈʌp wɪð/ (*past tense* & *past participle* put)
slow down /ˌsləʊ ˈdaʊn/
speed up /ˌspiːd ˈʌp/
take up /ˌteɪk ˈʌp (*past tense* took, *past participle* taken)

40 Giving your opinion

as far as I'm concerned /əz fɑː əz ˈaɪm kənˌsɜːnd/
I agree /aɪ əˈgriː/
I believe in /aɪ bɪˈliːv ɪn/
I disagree /aɪ ˌdɪsəˈgriː/
I have my doubts about /aɪ hæv maɪ ˈdaʊts əˌbaʊt/
I'm against /aɪm əˈgenst/
I'm in favour of /aɪm ɪn ˈfeɪvə əv/
in my opinion /ɪn ˈmaɪ əˌpɪnjən/
in my view /ɪn ˈmaɪ ˌvjuː/
I think /ˈaɪ ˌθɪŋk/
point of view /ˌpɔɪnt əv ˈvjuː/
to my mind /tə ˈmaɪ ˌmaɪnd/
What do you think of … ? /ˌwɒt duː juː ˌθɪŋk əv/
What do you think about … ? /ˌwɒt duː juː ˌθɪŋk əˌbaʊt/

Acknowledgements

I am very grateful to all the schools, institutions, teachers and students around the world who either piloted or commented on the material:

Katie Head, Cambridge, UK
Tadeusz Wolanski, Gdansk, Poland

I am also grateful to staff and students at the following institutions who tested the pilot material:

British Language Training Centre, Amsterdam, Netherlands
EPFC, Brussels, Belgium
Mercator-PCVD, Gent, Belgium
Sint Andreasinstitut, Bruges, Belgium

I would particularly like to thank Nóirín Burke and Martine Walsh at Cambridge University Press for all their help, guidance and support during the writing of this series. My thanks also to Liz Driscoll for her experienced editing of the material and to Jo Barker and Sarah Warburton for their excellent design and artwork.